FLASHBACK HISTORY

INUIT

Cherry and Bryan Alexander

Edited by Susie Brooks

PowerKiDS
press™

New York

Published in 2010 by The Rosen Publishing Group, Inc.
29 East 21st Street, New York, NY 10010

Copyright © 2010 Wayland/The Rosen Publishing Group, Inc.

First Edition

Original series design: Dave West
Designer and Illustrator: Celia Hart
Layout for this edition: Alix Wood
Editors for this edition: Susie Brooks and Katie Powell

Library of Congress Cataloging-in-Publication Data

Alexander, Cherry.
  Inuit / Cherry and Bryan Alexander.
     p. cm. — (Flashback history)
  Includes index.
  ISBN 978-1-4358-5507-6 (library binding) —
  ISBN 978-1-4358-5508-3 (pbk.) —
  ISBN 978-1-4358-5509-0 (6-pack)
 1. Inuit—History—Juvenile literature. 2. Inuit—Social life and customs—Juvenile literature. I. Alexander, Bryan. II. Title.
  E99.E7A4893 2010
  971.9004'9712—dc22

                         2009002626

Picture Credits: Robert Harding Picture Library, pp9(t), 36(t); Scott Polar Research Institute, p9(b); Tony Stone Images p43(c) (Daniel J. Cox); Valen photos,endpapers (Fred Breumer), p33(r) (John Eastcott/YVA Momatiuk). All other photographs by Bryan and Cherry Alexander.

Manufactured in China.

Endpapers: Inuit embroidery and appliqué work from St Jude's Anglican Cathedral, Iqaluit. It shows Inuit families with dogsleds and igloos.

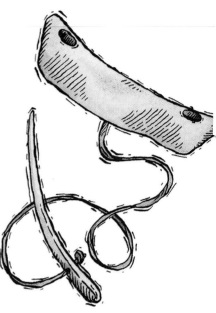

CONTENTS

Words that appear in
BOLD can be found in
the glossary on page 44.

WHO ARE THE INUIT?

The Inuit are natives of the icy Arctic—the area surrounding the North Pole. Their ancestors originally came from Asia, crossing the **Bering Land Bridge** into North America. Today, there are about 100,000 Inuit people, living across the Arctic regions of Siberia, Alaska, Canada, and Greenland. Before explorers arrived in the sixteenth century, the Inuit knew little of the rest of the world.

KEY

▪ Areas where the Inuit live

▫ Extent of summer sea ice

Permafrost tree line

LANDS ▶

For much of the year, the Arctic is covered in ice and snow. As this map shows, the Inuit live mainly near the coast. Here they can hunt animals and catch fish when the sea ice melts.

SIBERIA (RUSSIA)

BERING STRAIT

PACIFIC OCEAN

North Pole

GREENLAND
Thule
Qaanaaq ● Savissivik

Barrow

Prudhoe Bay

ALASKA

Tolman Island

Igloolik ● BAFFIN ISLAND

ATLANTIC OCEAN

Iqatuit

YUKON TERRITORY

Arctic Circle

Cape Dorset
Coral Harbour

NORTHWEST TERRITORIES

NUNAVUT

HUDSON BAY

Povungnituk

NEWFOUNDLAND

BRITISH COLUMBIA

CANADA

MANITOBA

QUEBEC

ALBERTA

ONTARIO

SASKATCHEWAN

USA

◀ HUNTER WITH DOGS

Tatigak hunts with a team of dogs. Like all Inuit, he is not very tall and his hands, feet, and nose are small. Having less surface area stops the Inuit from losing too much body heat in the cold. They still wear very thick furs in the winter.

POLAR LANDSCAPE ▲

Around the North Pole is an area where the ground 3 feet (1 meter) down never thaws. This is called permafrost and is marked by the **tree line** on the map. Some people say this is the true Arctic region.

POLAR EXPLORATION ▶

In 983 CE, a Viking named Eric the Red led a group of settlers to Greenland. He probably met the Inuit. This print shows a meeting in 1818 between the Inuit of northwest Greenland and two British sailors, Ross and Parry. They were looking for the Northwest Passage, a shortcut from Europe to the Pacific Ocean.

 INUIT OR ESKIMO?

You might have heard people call the Inuit "Eskimos." This name came from the **Algonquin Indians** of North America, and is thought to mean "eater of raw meat." It is still used in Siberia and western Alaska, where the Eskimos speak a language called Yupik. But in Canada and Greenland, most people prefer the name Inuit. This means "the people" in their native language **Inuktitut**. The word for one person is Inuk. Many Inuit and Eskimo groups have other names that they call themselves locally.

TIMELINE

	8000 BCE	3000–1000 BCE	1000 BCE–1000 CE	1000–1600	1600–1889	1890–1909
EVENTS IN THE ARCTIC	A group of Aleut people, distant relatives of the Inuit, cross the Bering Land Bridge. Some settle in Alaska, others move further inland.	Some Aleut move east from Alaska to Canada and Greenland. They start the "small tool tradition," which includes bows and arrows.	Descendants of the Aleut develop the "Dorset Culture," finding ways of hunting sea mammals. They spread east from Alaska to Siberia and west to Greenland. They extend the small tool culture.	This is a mild, ice-free period. Ancestors of today's Inuit, called the Thule people, move along the north of Canada to Greenland, hunting whales in the sea.	1721 A Norwegian priest, Hans Egede, brings Christianity to Greenland. 1870s Visiting whalers kill so many whales and walrus that Alaskans nearly starve.	1903–1906 Norwegian explorer Roald Amundsen discovers the Northwest Passage. 1909 The U.S. explorer Robert Peary reaches the North Pole after several attempts.
EVENTS IN NORTH AMERICA	17000–7000 BCE The Bering Land Bridge joins Asia and North America. **Woolly mammoth**			1000 The Viking explorer Leif Ericson discovers America. 1492 The Italian explorer Christopher Columbus arrives in America.		1898 The engine-driven submarine is invented.
EVENTS IN EUROPE	Huge ice sheets from the last Ice Age start to disappear from Northern Europe. Forests grow and people hunt and gather food.	1700 BCE The Bronze Age starts in Western Europe.	983 CE The Viking explorer Eric the Red discovers Greenland. 1066 The Normans invade Britain at Hastings.	1347–1391 The Black Death, or plague, sweeps across Europe and kills up to half of the population.	1789 The French Revolution takes place. 1859 The English naturalist Charles Darwin writes *Origin of Species*, a book that includes his theory on how human life began.	
EVENTS AROUND THE WORLD	4000 BCE The potter's wheel is invented in Mesopotamia. 3760 BCE The Jewish calendar begins.	**Tutankhamun's death mask** 1352 BCE King Tutankhamun dies in Ancient Egypt.	236 BCE Building starts on the Great Wall of China.	1000 The Chinese invent gunpowder. 1272 Marco Polo visits China.		**Queen Victoria** 1891 Work starts on the Trans-Siberian Railway, a route connecting Moscow in Russia to the Pacific coast.

1910–1949	1950–1979	1980–1999	1999-2009
1921–1924 A Danish explorer, Knud Rasmussen, visits and documents nearly all of the Inuit groups in Arctic America.	1953 The building of Thule Air Base in Greenland moves 116 Inuit from their homes. 1979 Greenland gains home rule from Denmark.	1982 The European Community bans imports of seal products. 1999 Nunavut, an Inuit-governed territory, is established in Canada.	Melting ice caps highlight the effects of **global warming**. 2007 The Northwest Passage is completely ice-free for the first time since records began.
1927 A U.S. pilot, Charles Lindbergh, flies nonstop across the Atlantic. 1939 Canada enters into World War II. 1941 The U.S. joins World War II after Japan attacks Pearl harbor.	**Buddy Holly** 1959 Buddy Holly, a rock-and-roll star, dies in a plane crash.	1982 Canada gains independence from the U.K.	2001 Almost 3,000 people die in terror attacks, now known as 9/11. 2005 Hurricane Katrina causes severe floods in New Orleans.
	1961 The Berlin Wall is built.	1986 The first triple organ transplant of heart, lungs, and liver takes place in the U.K. 1994 The Channel Tunnel opens between France and England.	2002 European national currencies are replaced by the Euro. 2007 Gordon Brown succeeds Tony Blair as U.K. Prime Minister.
1948 The South African government introduces Apartheid, separating the lives of black and white people.	1957–1975 The Vietnam War takes place. 1974 The Terracotta Army is unearthed near Xian, China.	1991 Communist rule ends in the U.S.S.R. 1994 Nelson Mandela becomes the first black South African president. 1997 The UN sets targets to tackle climate change.	2003 An Ice Bike is trialed in the Antarctic as a new means of Polar travel. 2008 There are roughly 1,500 million Internet users worldwide (about 22 per cent of the total population).

THULE CULTURE

The Thule people were named after Thule in northwest Greenland, where their first remains were found. They probably came from north Alaska around 1000 CE and quickly spread east, across northern Canada. In those days, the Arctic was warmer and the seas were full of life. The Thule most likely followed bowhead whales, killing enough in the summer months to feed them through the winter. In about 1200 CE, the climate started to cool and many Thule died. Survivors had to find new ways to live and hunt in the harsher climate.

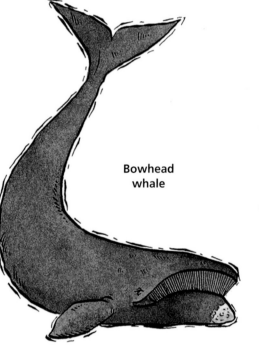

Bowhead whale

DOGSLEDS

Clues among the remains of the Thule culture show they used dogs for hunting. **Archaeologists** have found bones drilled into the shape of sled runners as well as long whip handles.

WHERE DO THE INUIT GET THEIR FOOD?

Crops won't grow in the freezing Arctic, so the Inuit rely on killing animals for food. Most Inuit groups hunt seals, polar bears, and walrus. Some also find **caribou** and **musk oxen**. The Inuit eat a lot of fish, which they catch through holes cut into the ice. There are stores which sell food shipped in from the south, but this is expensive. Often, Inuit families buy what they call "country food" from their neighbors who hunt.

◀ AN INUK SETS HIS SEAL NET

In the early fall, the sea ice is still thin after the summer thaw. Some Inuit set seal nets under the ice, usually where the water is fast-flowing. They visit the nets regularly to remove any seals they have caught. Seal meat is an important part of the Inuit diet.

 101 USES FOR A DEAD CARIBOU

The early Inuit relied heavily on caribou. They ate the animal's meat and used its skin to make tents, bedding, and clothing. They sewed using **sinews** for thread, with needles carved out of caribou bones. Antlers became spears, arrowheads, and even snow goggles!

INUK HUNTER WITH A CARIBOU ▲

This Inuk tracked down a caribou herd and shot this animal using a high-powered rifle. Caribou meat is very high in protein and low in fat. It will provide an almost complete diet, as long as the liver is eaten, too. The only thing that is missing is Vitamin D, which the Inuit get from fish.

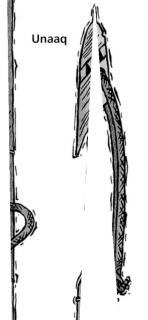

Kakivak

Unaaq

INUK FISHING ▶

An Inuk fisherman has to dig through a lot of snow before he can cut a hole in the ice. He dips a small bait into the water and moves it up and down until a fish bites.

◀ HUNTING TOOLS

Sometimes fish are caught using nets, hooks, or a three-pronged spear called a kakivak. The unaaq is another traditional spear, or **harpoon**, with a long rope attached to a sealskin or rubber float. This is still used in northwest Greenland, where laws say that some animals must be harpooned before they are shot.

FOOD SHOPPING IN AN ICY LAND ▲

Local food stores save the Inuit from starving when hunting is bad. But things that spoil, like milk or fruit, cost a lot because they come from so far away. "Country foods" such as Caribou are cheaper, and often more nutritious.

DO THE INUIT EAT WELL?

Medical research has shown that the Inuit are very healthy. Few suffer from illnesses such as cancer, diabetes, or heart disease. Their meaty diet is high in protein and good fats, as well as vitamins. Who needs oranges when whale skin and seal liver contain just as much Vitamin C? In times of plenty, the Inuit dry, bury, or freeze food to keep it. In the summer, they eat plants, flowers, and berries. They also fish from inland lakes.

EATING RAW SEAL LIVER ▶

Eating handfuls of raw, bleeding seal liver is nothing new for these Inuit girls. It is quicker not to cook the meat, especially when they are out on a hunting trip. A favorite Inuit food is *mukuk*, a chewy layer of gristle from the **narwhal**. The Inuit cut it into bite-size pieces and eat it with their fingers with salt. Meats like this are higher in Vitamin C when they are raw.

"I would like to say a few words about this land. The only food I like is meat."
Salluviniq, Resolute Bay.

◀ HANGING UP FISH TO DRY

Fish are good for the Inuit because they contain Vitamin D. In the summer, fishing for Arctic char is popular. The Inuit find lakes that are still partly frozen, so they can fish in the deepest waters without a boat. To dry their catch, they remove the bones and make criss-cross cuts in the flesh. Then they hang the fish up until all the moisture has gone. In the winter, a sack of dried char makes a nice change from seal meat or caribou.

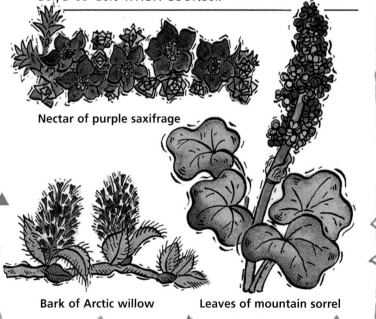

CATCHING BIRDS ▲

Little auks are small seabirds that flock to the Arctic in the spring. They fly very fast and are hard to catch. The Inuit sweep them up in long-handled nets. Auk can be eaten raw or cooked, or buried inside sealskins for many months to make a delicacy called *kaviak*.

DANGEROUS FOODS

There are some foods that the Inuit know not to eat. For example, polar bear liver contains so much Vitamin A that it is poisonous. Even the **huskies** must not eat it. Some animals, including polar bear and walrus, can also have parasites, or worms. Their meat is only safe to eat when cooked.

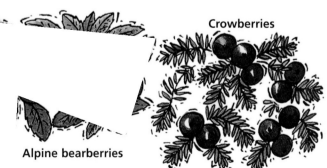

Crowberries

Alpine bearberries

Nectar of purple saxifrage

COLLECTING PLANTS AND BERRIES ▲

Summer offers the Inuit a rare chance to eat their greens. These pictures show some of the foods they get from Arctic plants, including nectar and bark.

Bark of Arctic willow

Leaves of mountain sorrel

HOW DO THE INUIT SURVIVE THE COLD?

During the Arctic winter, temperatures can dip as low as -58 °F (-50°C). In some areas, the sun sets in late October and won't rise again until February. The months are dark and cold, but the Inuit still hunt. They often travel a long way, tracking walrus, and polar bears. In the summer, the sea thaws for a few weeks, but in places, a thin layer of ice remains.

◀ SUMMER HUNTING

In the summer, the sun stays in the sky for 24 hours a day. The sea comes to life and birds from as far away as the South Pole come to feed and breed. The Inuit hunt from **kayaks** on the ice-free water. They catch narwhals using a throwing board to lever a harpoon through the air. Harpooning whales rather than just shooting them means that fewer get killed.

POLAR NIGHT AND MIDNIGHT SUN ▼

You can see from these diagrams why the poles have continuous daylight in the summer and continuous darkness in the winter.

The Earth spins around the sun at an angle. In June, the North Pole faces the sun. In December, it points away.

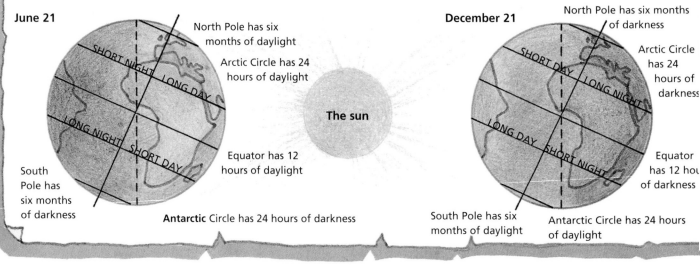

June 21

SHORT NIGHT — LONG DAY
LONG NIGHT — SHORT DAY

North Pole has six months of daylight

Arctic Circle has 24 hours of daylight

South Pole has six months of darkness

Equator has 12 hours of daylight

The sun

Antarctic Circle has 24 hours of darkness

December 21

SHORT DAY — LONG NIGHT
LONG DAY — SHORT NIGHT

North Pole has six months of darkness

Arctic Circle has 24 hours of darkness

Equator has 12 hours of darkness

South Pole has six months of daylight

Antarctic Circle has 24 hours of daylight

◀ INUIT RUNNING TO KEEP WARM

It can be very cold sitting on a sled, even if you're wrapped in thick fur clothing. The Inuit often run behind their sleds to get the blood pumping back to their fingers and toes. When they are warm enough, they sit down again.

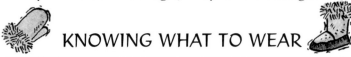

KNOWING WHAT TO WEAR

The Inuit are experts at dressing for the cold. Early Antarctic explorers used to visit them to buy clothing, before heading south to the opposite end of the Earth. The secret is to borrow from nature, which has given Arctic animals the snuggest winter coats. Caribou fur is warm because every hair is hollow and traps the air in a cosy layer. Although polar bears look white, their hair is actually clear. This draws sunlight down to their black skin, which soaks up and keeps in the heat.

SNOW-COVERED HUSKY ▼

The Inuit use husky dogs to pull their sleds. Huskies have thick fur, but when they get really cold, they curl up into a tight ball. Their tail wraps snugly over their feet and nose, and they can sleep soundly under a blanket of storm-driven snow.

PUTTING BOOTS ON HUSKIES ▲

When the sea ice starts to melt in summer, sharp needles form on its surface. These can cut the huskies' paws. The Inuit make dog boots from pieces of oilskin or canvas. They cut holes for the claws, so the huskies can get a good grip on the slippery ground.

DO THE INUIT HAVE FAMILIES LIKE OURS?

Most Inuit families are like ours, with mother, father, and children living in one house. Some share their homes with an older relative, whose experience in sewing or making hunting tools is highly valued. Inuit hunters marry as soon as they can. They need a wife to clean their sealskins and make their clothes. This is hard work, and many Inuit girls today would prefer to marry men with better-paid jobs in the towns.

MOTHER WITH CHILD ▼

A Mother carries her baby in an *amaut* like this for the first year. The baby gets warmth from her back. Disposable diapers keep a baby dry, but traditionally, moss was used.

EXTENDED HUNTING FAMILY ▲

Up to 16 people live in this hunting hut on Baffin Island, where there is often good caribou hunting in the winter. While the men hunt, the women clean skins and do chores. Everyone shares the work, and the meat!

◀ ITUKU AND PANERAK AT HOME

In their one-roomed house, Ituku holds his son Igayak while his wife Panerak softens a piece of sealskin. Inuit children grow up seeing their parents feeding dogs and working with skins. When they are ready, they'll learn these skills in order to become hunters themselves.

NUK WITH HIS GRANDSON ▶

Family is very important to the Inuit. This man and his grandson spend as much time together as they can. Grandparents will often adopt a grandchild if there is any problem with the parents looking after him or her.

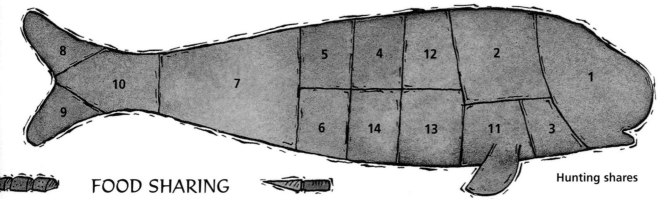

Hunting shares

FOOD SHARING

When the Inuit go out hunting, there is always a danger that they won't find enough food. In the past, old people were sometimes left behind to starve in a bad year. Parents would even kill their own babies rather than see them die of hunger. By sharing food, the Inuit hope to avoid this awful fate. Good hunters have always shared their meat with less skilled family members, and everyone gets part of the kill on a hunting trip. Hunters know they need to bring home enough meat for the whole village—including the huskies.

HUNTING SHARES ▲

You can see here how a whale might be divided among hunters. Parts 1, 2, 3, and 10, plus the heart and **intestines**, go to the harpooner. The second harpooner, if there is one, gets parts 7, 8, and 9. The rest is shared by others who helped to spear the whale or tow it ashore. Very little of an animal is wasted.

DO THE INUIT LIVE IN HOUSES?

In the past, a few Inuit groups lived in igloos over the winter, but most  built turf houses that were easy to keep warm. They moved from place to place, following the best hunting grounds. Today, most Inuit live in settled communities. These are often a long way from the good hunting. Many Inuit rely on payments from the government to survive.

BUILDING AN IGLOO ▶

To build an igloo, an Inuk saws blocks out of snow. These are shaped with a knife and laid in a spiral, gradually leaning in to form a dome. Traditionally, there were many types of igloo. Some were simple shelters, and others had lots of rooms. In parts of Canada, children learn igloo building at school.

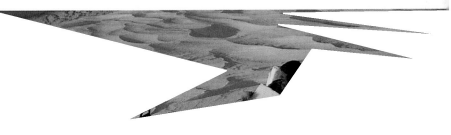

INSIDE AN IGLOO ▲

This Inuk from Greenland is lighting a stove to cook on and warm his igloo.

IGLOO AT NIGHT ▲

An igloo provides good shelter against the wind. Air trapped in the walls keeps it warm inside.

SAVISSIVIK, AN INUIT VILLAGE ▲

Savissivik is a modern Inuit village, with houses made of timber from the south. Unlike traditional Inuit homes, these have separate bedrooms and are larger and harder to heat. They are raised off the permafrost on stilts.

TURF HOUSE ▶

Turf houses varied depending on local materials. In Alaska, people layered the turf with whalebone and wood, but elsewhere rocks were used. The houses were small, with an underground entrance to stop heat from escaping. They were cheap and easy to build, so families could have one in each of their hunting areas.

Turf house

INSIDE A MODERN HOUSE ▶

This modern Inuit house has electricity, central heating, and space to stand up and walk around. Televisions, phones, email, and radios have also become a part of Inuit life.

WHAT DO THE INUIT WEAR?

The Inuit are good at protecting themselves against the snow and biting winds. They know exactly what makes the warmest clothes. Until white people came to the Arctic, the Inuit had no woven fabrics. Today, they can shop for woolen clothes, but they still prefer to wear skins and furs outside. The type they use depends on the animals they hunt.

SOFTENING SKINS BY CHEWING ▲

This Inuk woman is chewing a piece of dried sealskin, to soften it for a pair of boots. She uses her front teeth so the skin doesn't get soggy. Lots of older women have worn down their teeth by doing this for many years. Dentists have suggested they hammer the skin instead, but this damages the skin so it is not properly waterproof.

INUK DRESSED IN FURS ▲

Kigutikak is wearing *nannuk* – polar bear skin trousers. His *qulittaq* is a caribou fur coat, with a blue foxfur trim on the hood. The sealskin boots, or *kamik*, have bearded sealskin soles. Inside is a sock of sheepskin or fur from an Arctic hare.

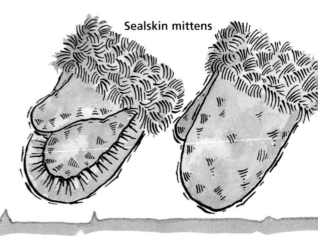

Sealskin mittens

◄ MODERN DRESS

It makes sense to dress children in man-made clothes that are easy to clean. The Inuit can buy these in local stores. Everyone but the oldest in the village wears modern clothing most of the time. Inuit who head out for long periods in the winter will usually put on furs.

THERMAL UNDERWEAR

The Inuit can now buy the latest thermal underwear. But in the past, they used natural materials. Undershirts were made from the skin of sea birds, with the feathers on the inside. Arctic hare skin was turned into socks. There were problems. All these items tore easily and couldn't be washed.

DRYING SKIN ▼

Skins are stretched out to dry on a frame like this once they have been cleaned. The fur may be left on or removed.

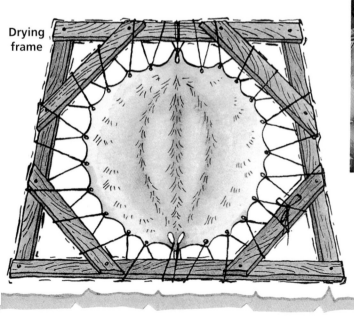

Drying frame

WOMAN MAKING BOOTS ▲

Traditional boots are no longer sewn with *ivaluq*, a thread made from dried narwhal sinews. Today's Inuit use dental floss instead!

DO THE INUIT GO TO WORK?

Inuit hunting families work very hard. In the past, they found all they needed on the land and did not expect to be paid. Hunters still catch food and get water from melted ice. But they also need money for goods such as fuel, bullets, and toilet paper. When people in the south stopped buying seal and fox skins, many Inuit hunting families suffered. Life is easier for those with jobs, because they earn money to buy what they need.

INUK FEEDING DOGS ▲

An Inuk feeds more meat to his dogs than to his family. He may have up to 15 huskies, but he must be a good hunter to keep a big team. During the winter, the dogs eat every other day. A meal of raw walrus meat takes a long time to digest and provides enough energy for long journeys. In the summer, the huskies rest and are fed less often.

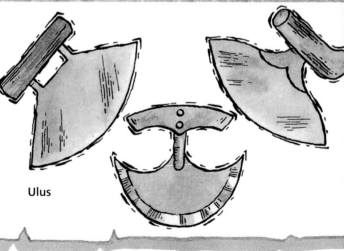

Ulus

WORKING DAYS

The Inuit are ruled by the seasons in the Arctic. The changeable weather and long winter darkness make it difficult for them to work nine-to-five. Some Inuit say, "The wind carries sleep," because during a storm they often stay inside and doze. In the summer, when the sun stays in the sky, they make up for lost time. Inuit hunters rarely separate work and leisure. A lot of effort is needed just to keep everyone fed and clothed.

WOMAN CARRYING ICE ▲

Collecting ice is a woman's job, and it can be very slow. Icebergs, which provide fresh water, are often a long way from the village.

CLEANING A SKIN ▲

Panerak is scraping fat off of a sealskin. She takes care not to make any holes. Her "woman's knife," called an *ulu* (left), is kept very sharp. She uses it for cutting meat, too.

WORKING IN A STORE ▲

There are one or two stores in each small Inuit village. This Inuk is moving soft drinks from the storeroom to the shelves. He earns cash, but he may still choose to hunt on the weekends.

WHAT DO THE INUIT DO IN THEIR SPARE TIME?

Most of the time, the Inuit are busy hunting, making clothes, and heating their homes. But of course they have fun, too. During bad weather or long winter nights, families like telling stories about exciting hunts or things that make them laugh. The Inuit have a good community spirit and everyone loves visiting their neighbors. Playing the skin drum was a traditional Inuit pastime, but now their music is much more varied.

STRING PUZZLES ▼

Mikisuk is making an *ajarraaq*, or string puzzle, of a tent. Her grandmother showed her how to do this. Traditionally, the Inuit used a thong of sealskin instead of string. Some Inuit puzzles are very complicated and have stories or rhymes to go with them. Many other cultures around the world make string puzzles, too.

VISITING WITH A TEACUP ▲

Saufak used to always take a teacup when she visited her neighbors, in case they didn't have one spare. In the 1940s, the Inuit did this to avoid catching tuberculosis. This disease is now present in the Arctic again, so people have to be very careful. Visiting is an important part of village life. It keeps relationships strong.

◀ PLAYING ON THE ICE

These children are playing a risky game on broken sea ice. If they fall into the water, they could be swept under the ice and drown. The water is close to or below 32°F (0°C). Children need to learn how to deal with the different types of ice at a young age.

Ajagaq

GAMES AND PASTIMES ▶

Inuit games are useful for testing skills. The *ajagaq* needs good coordination to toss a large bone and land one of its holes over a spike. Tug-of-war handles, made of wood and a sealskin strap, test the strength of two people sitting on the ground.

GIRL PLAYING A GUITAR ▼

Some Inuit children learn to play modern musical instruments. With a guitar, they can play the songs of an **Inuhuit** band called "Flying Kayak." This group is popular in Greenland.

Tug-of-war handles

THE CHANGE IN GAMES

Inuit children can now buy frisbees and plastic footballs at shops. But the Inuit have always been clever at creating things from scraps. Balls used to be made of seal bladders, blown up and left to dry. Bones from seal flippers were turned into a game like jacks.

DO BOYS AND GIRLS GO TO SCHOOL?

Inuit children once roamed the land with their families, learning all they needed to by copying the adults around them. In the 1950s, the Canadian government introduced laws that meant all Inuit children had to go to school. Parents finally settled in villages to be near the schools. Children started to learn about life in the south from books.

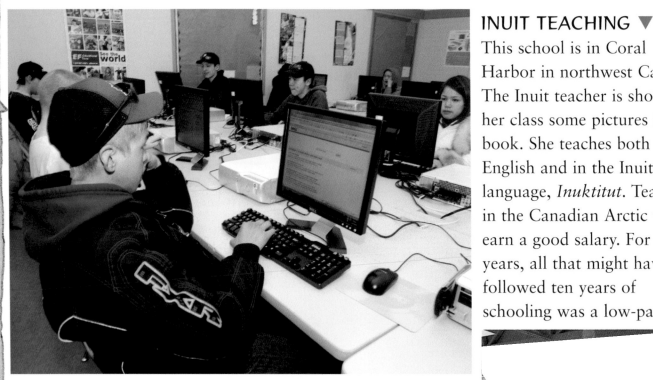

A BOY USING A COMPUTER ▲

In the Canadian north, schools have computers that work in both Inuktitut and English. They also have excellent indoor sports facilities. Girls learn traditional skills, such as beadwork and sewing sealskins, as well as standard lessons. Inuit children today are well educated in both their own culture and that of the modern world.

INUIT TEACHING ▼

This school is in Coral Harbor in northwest Canada. The Inuit teacher is showing her class some pictures in a book. She teaches both in English and in the Inuit's own language, *Inuktitut*. Teachers in the Canadian Arctic today earn a good salary. For many years, all that might have followed ten years of schooling was a low-paid job.

Sewing thimble

Needle, thread, and beads

◀ MAKING A SLED

Boys at this school in Savissivik are learning to make a traditional sled. They join the wooden pieces with cords instead of nails for flexibility.

HUNTING WITH FATHER ▼

The day a boy kills his first seal is very important. His father shows him how to stalk a sleeping seal by holding up a white cotton screen. When he has crept close enough, he shoots.

LANGUAGE AND SYLLABICS ▼

Inuktitut wasn't taught in the first Arctic schools. Most of the teachers were white and spoke English, which the children did not understand. Today, most communities have Inuit teachers. Inuktitut is considered important to the culture. It is written in shapes called syllabics, each of which represents a sound. Getting a triangle in slightly the wrong position can change the meaning of a word completely!

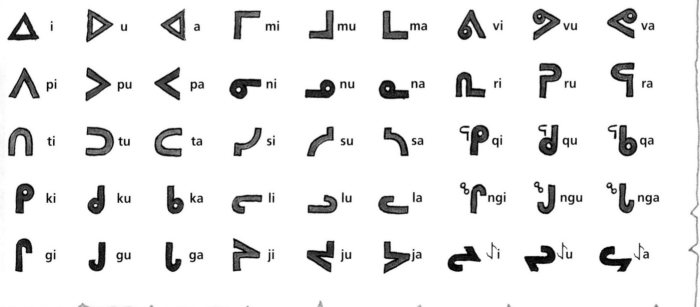

◁ i	▷ u	◁ a	Γ mi	⌐ mu	L ma	⋀ vi	⟩ vu	⟨ va
⋀ pi	⟩ pu	⟨ pa	⌐ ni	⌐ nu	⌐ na	⌐ ri	⌐ ru	⌐ ra
∩ ti	⊃ tu	⊂ ta	⌐ si	⌐ su	⌐ sa	⌐ qi	⌐ qu	⌐ qa
P ki	⌐ ku	⌐ ka	⌐ li	⌐ lu	⌐ la	⌐ ngi	⌐ ngu	⌐ nga
Γ gi	J gu	L ga	⌐ ji	⌐ ju	⌐ ja	⌐ √i	⌐ √u	⌐ √a

ARE THE INUIT ARTISTS?

The Inuit have always created beautiful things, but not necessarily for art. Archaeologists have found tiny figures that might have been children's toys or lucky charms. Today, Inuit artists make prints and carvings to sell to people in the south. Popular subjects include Arctic wildlife and characters from local stories.

MABEL MAKES A PRINT ▲

Mabel Nigiyak is working on a design that her daughter will make into a stone-cut print. They will print a limited number of copies. Collectors in the south love this kind of art. A yearly catalog tells them what is available.

PITSEOLAK

Pitseolak was a famous Inuit artist from Baffin Island in Canada. When she was very old, someone asked her why she painted. She said, "Firstly, I did it for the money, but now I hope that when I die I can continue to paint in Heaven."

◀ INUK CARVES IN STONE

Nukapianguak is sculpting an Inuit hunter out of hard Greenlandic stone. Most artists use soapstone because it is much softer and easier to carve.

Decorated hunting coat

DECORATED COATS ▲

The Copper Inuit, from the western Arctic, decorate their hunting coats with a "delta trim." This is a pattern made from light and dark pieces of caribou skin. It takes about a month to sew enough trim for the bottom of a coat.

◀ THE LEGEND CARVINGS

In 1958, the Canadian Inuit of Povungnituk started carving their local legends in soapstone. They were the first to sell their art for money. This soapstone shows an Inuk wrestling with a *tuniq*.

DO THE INUIT WRITE BOOKS?

The Inuit passed on all their history by word of mouth, until **missionaries** arrived in the Arctic. Canadian missionaries invented the Inuktitut symbols (see page 29), while in Greenland they used the alphabet we recognize. Inuit stories could finally be written down. Now the Inuit read comics, books, and newspapers in both Greenlandic and syllabic.

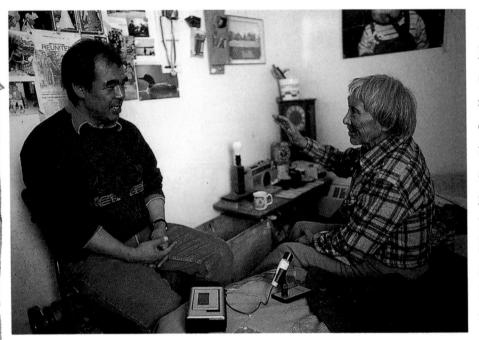

◀ RECORDING STORIES

Many elderly Inuit, like Noah (on the right), recorded stories about their younger days. They tell of times when there were no settled villages and fearless hunters faced ghosts in their huts. Some tales, called myths, explain how things like the sun and moon came into being. Recording them means they won't be forgotten.

A TRADITIONAL STORY

In the olden days, all birds were white. Then one day the Raven and the Loon decided to draw patterns on each other's feathers. The Raven went first, but the Loon was so unhappy with the result that it spat black paint all over the Raven. Since that day, all ravens have been black. The Raven was so angry that it beat the Loon about the legs until it could hardly walk. And that is why the loon is such an awkward bird on land.

Loon

Raven

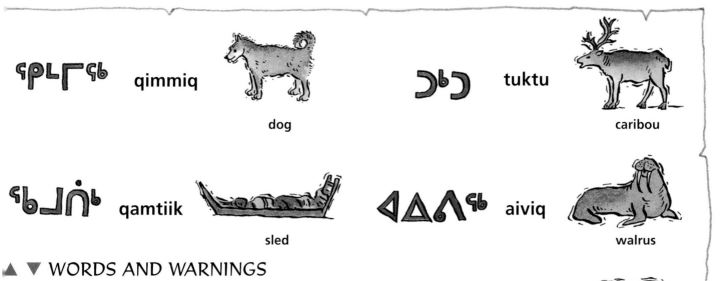

ᕿᒻᒥᖅ qimmiq
dog

ᖃᒧᑏᒃ qamtiik
sled

ᑐᒃᑐ tuktu
caribou

ᐊᐃᕖᖅ aiviq
walrus

ᓇᓄᖅ nanuq
polar bear

▲ ▼ WORDS AND WARNINGS

Above, you can see some common Inuktitut words. Below is a warning sign on a building in Canada. Since some Inuit do not understand English or French, it includes syllabics.

☀ SPREADING MYTHS ◐

Inuit communities from Siberia to Greenland have many similar myths and stories. This shows how well word of mouth works. One popular myth tells the story of Sedna, the powerful spirit of the sea. She is usually described as a beautiful girl who refuses to accept a husband, until she is tricked into marrying a dog or a bird. One day she falls out of a kayak, and when she tries to climb back in her fingers are cut off. Sedna sinks to the bottom of the ocean. Her fingers become all the creatures of the sea and she rules over them forever more. Sedna is often pictured rather like a mermaid, with a human head and the tail of a whale or seal.

GIRL ON COMPUTER ▼

The Inuit tradition of storytelling still goes on in some villages. But now that the Inuit have books and computers, families spend less time sitting around sharing tales.

DO THE INUIT GO TO THE DOCTOR?

Few Inuit villages have a doctor's surgery, but most have a nurse. Doctors visit often to make sure everyone is healthy. If someone is seriously ill, they are flown to a hospital in one of the towns. Dentists and opticians may visit several times a year. Like doctors, they travel by dogsled, or since the 1950s, by air ambulance.

DOCTOR'S VISIT ▲

This doctor is visiting Tabatha's family at a hunting camp. He will check everyone's health and give the baby his vaccinations. The nearest town with a hospital is a day away by dogsled or boat.

CAUGHT IN THE MIDDLE

The government encouraged the Inuit to settle in villages because they believed it would be safer and better for them. For example, it would be easier to set up a system of medical care and good schools. But forcing the Inuit to change their traditional way of life brought its own problems. Many Inuit have struggled to find well-paid work—and in the villages they need money to survive. Troubled times have led to sad stories in most of the larger communities, including suicides, crimes related to alcohol, and recently, drug abuse.

MEDICINE CALL ▼

If someone is sick, the village nurse can contact a doctor by radio. The doctor tells her which medicines to use.

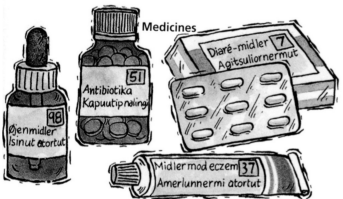

Medicines

Øjenmidler
Isinut atortut `98`

Antibiotika
Kapuutipnaling `51`

Diaré-midler `7`
Agitsuliornermut

Midler mod eczem `37`
Amerlunnermi atortut

A FLYING DENTIST ▲

This dentist has just arrived at a village in northern Greenland. Flying is quicker than sledding, and it is easier to land a helicopter than a plane on the rough ground. Fixed-wing planes are used throughout the Canadian Arctic. In an emergency, pilots will brave the worst weathers to save a life.

WHALER DISEASES ▶

After 1850, whalers visited the Arctic each year to hunt. Sometimes they brought with them killer diseases and infections, such as smallpox, tuberculosis, measles, and influenza. In some Inuit communities, up to half the people died from these infections.

DO THE INUIT BELIEVE IN LIFE AFTER DEATH?

The Inuit believe that when people die, their soul divides in two. One part goes to a place where there is always warmth and good hunting. The other stays on Earth until a new baby is given the same name. Most Inuit today are Christians, but older generations believed strongly in spirits. They had rules, called taboos, to keep the spirits happy. A person called an angakkuq, or **shaman**, communicated with the spirit world.

CHRISTIANITY ▶

In 1721, a Norwegian priest, Hands Egede, was the first of many missionaries to arrive in the Arctic. These religious teachers wanted the Inuit to give up their beliefs and turn to Christianity instead. Bit by bit, they broke down the faith in shamans and taboos. This had a big impact on the Inuit culture.

◀ GRAVES IN THE SNOW

It is very hard to bury anything in snowy **tundra** lands. As the ground thaws and refreezes each year, the largest objects come to the surface. Bones rise to the top of graves in this way. They are always treated with great respect. Traditionally, the Inuhuit would sew a dead body into a skin and drag it to face the rising sun. Then they would bury it under rocks, along with the person's belongings.

DRUM SINGING ▲

All Inuit groups practice drum singing and dancing. It has long been used for ceremonies, entertainment, and even to settle arguments — the best drummer was always right!

TABOOS

Spirits and taboos gave the Inuit guidance through life. Breaking a taboo, even by mistake, was thought to bring bad luck. The Inuit tried to please powerful spirits such as Sedna, who had control over sea animals and bad weather. They believed that all creatures had souls, so when a hunter killed an animal he would offer it gifts of food and water. He hoped that this kindness would bring him more animals to hunt in future—when Sedna's creatures were happy they did not mind giving themselves up to provide meat, clothes and shelter for the Inuit.

TUPILAKS ▼

Tupilaks are monsters carved from ivory. For 5,000 years, the Inuit believed they would become real and get rid of enemies. Now tupilaks are sold as souvenirs.

Tupilaks

HOW DO THE INUIT TRAVEL?

Zipping across the snow on a husky-drawn sled is a great way to travel in the winter. In the summer, when the sea ice melts, the Inuit get around by boat. They may hunt in a kayak, a traditional type of canoe. The umiak is a larger open boat that can fit a whole family inside. Today's Inuit have modern motorboats and snowmobiles. There are also air links between major towns.

DOGSLEDS ON A LONG HUNT ▲

These hunters are returning from a long polar bear hunt. When the sun comes up in February, they can travel huge distances from home. Dogsleds help them to venture far out onto the ice to find the best hunting. The strong huskies pull heavy loads of meat back to the village.

◄ KAYAK

Kayaks are made from a wooden frame covered in sealskin or canvas. This Inuk has built his own. He measured it to suit his exact shape and height.

UMIAK ▶

Nowadays umiaks are used only in northern Alaska and Siberia, by Inuit hunting walrus and bowhead whales. These flat-bottomed boats have walrus skin stretched over their wooden frame. They are light enough to be pulled up onto the ice. The Inuit use oars or sails to power them through the water.

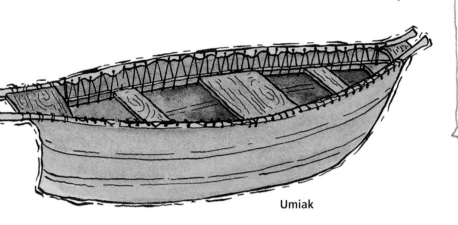
Umiak

SNOWMOBILES ▲

In the early days, snowmobiles were unreliable and were often known as "ride out and walk homes." Today, many Canadian Inuit use them all the time. Snowmobiles are more expensive to run than dogsleds, but they are quicker and can cover more ground. Because of this, many areas close to the villages have been **overhunted**.

TRAFFIC RESTRICTIONS

Some 30 years ago, the Inuhuit of Greenland saw the bad effects that motor vehicles were having in other parts of the Arctic. They decided to make new rules to protect local wildlife and their culture at the same time. They banned the use of snowmobiles for hunting, and also made some areas of water into motorboat-free zones. As a result, wildlife in Greenland has not been overhunted as in other parts of the Arctic.

HOW HAVE WE AFFECTED THE LIVES OF THE INUIT?

We may live far away from the Inuit, but our lives still have an impact on theirs. Pollution from modern industries, homes, and vehicles is carried all the way to the Arctic and has poisoned many hunting grounds. The polar ice is melting as global warming takes its toll. In addition, trade in sealskins is now banned or restricted in many parts of the world. All this has made survival for the Inuit very hard.

SAVING SEALS ▶

From the 1960s onward, people became concerned about the killing of baby harp seals for their fluffy white coats. In fact, it was Canadians south of the Arctic who were killing the babies—the Inuit hunt only older seals. But campaigns led to restrictions on skin trading across the United States and Europe. This meant a huge loss of business for the Inuit.

◀ TOXIC POLAR BEARS

These scientists are examining a sedated polar bear. They can work out its age from its teeth and its weight from length and chest measurements. By taking samples of blood and fat, they can tell how pollution is affecting these animals. Scientists have found high levels of poison in polar bears.

Before the Inuit met white people, they knew how to make the best of local materials. But when traders arrived, they introduced products that couldn't be found in the Arctic. Soon the Inuit's lives changed and they wanted things that only money could buy. Now they need regular work to pay for goods such as motor vehicles, TVs, and DVDs.

LASTING LITTER ▲

The U.S. military left these oil drums at an old radar station in Canada. Rubbish like this will not rot in the cold, dry Arctic air.

NEW BAN ▶

Many countries still allow some trade in adult sealskins, as long as the animals are humanely killed. But in 2008, the **European Union** considered a total ban. This is another huge worry for the Inuit.

It's my world too!

INTERNATIONAL
FUND FOR
ANIMAL WELFARE

◀ OIL IN ALASKA

Modern life has brought many oil and mining companies to the Arctic. Oil is pumped from this production plant in Prudhoe Bay, Alaska, to be distributed all over the world. The Inuit have to compete with people from the south over jobs and rights to the land. They also fear for the damage that the oil industry is doing to their environment.

WHAT IS HAPPENING TO THE INUIT?

Today's Inuit have a lot of independence. In 1999, a territory called Nunavut, meaning "our land," was created in Canada's eastern Arctic. This gave the Inuit ownership of 135,135 square miles (350,000 square kilometers) of land—an area about the size of Norway. The Inuit run their own affairs, such as education, wildlife management, and land use. They also have their own TV and radio stations, with programs in Inuktitut.

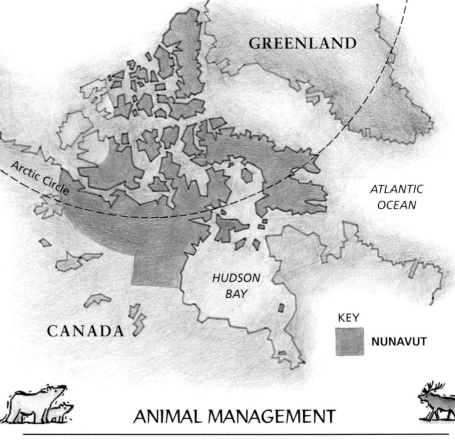

MORE CONTROL ▶

Nunavut has given the Inuit a much-needed boost. After 150 years of being told how to run their lives, they can now make the most of their great local knowledge. Today's Inuit have better job opportunities in areas such as mining, oil and gas, and government services. Tourism brings employment and helps the native art and culture to thrive. The Inuit Circumpolar Conference, set up in 1977, brings Inuit groups together. They meet every three years to discuss problems and work toward a happy future.

ANIMAL MANAGEMENT

Many Arctic animals are seriously threatened by global warming and overhunting. Throughout the Arctic, Inuit people are working with scientists to monitor wildlife populations. The Inuit help with samples and trapping, and in return, they receive information about animal numbers and the environment. This helps them to decide how, what, and where it is best to hunt.

INUK TELEVISION ▲

TV and radio programs help to keep the Inuktitut language alive. They broadcast local news and other features that keep the Inuit in touch with the rest of the world.

INUK "MOUNTIE" ▲

This Inuk Royal Canadian Mounted Policeman has a big truck and uniform to show his authority. He understands local people and problems better than a non-native would.

CLIMATE CHANGE ▶

One major concern for the Inuit today is climate change. Temperatures are rising all over the world, but especially in the polar regions. Arctic winters are no longer as long or as cold as they were, and hunting becomes increasingly difficult on the thinning ice.

"We cannot pass on our traditional knowledge, because it is no longer reliable. Before, I could look at cloud patterns or the wind, or even what stars are twinkling, and predict the weather. Now, everything is changed."

Donald Mearns, an Inuk.

"We have lived in this region for centuries and we will continue to. As the climate changes, we will adapt."

Theo Ikumaq, an Inuk.

GLOSSARY

ALGONQUIN INDIANS Native North Americans living south of the Arctic area, who speak the Algonquin language.

ANTARCTIC The region around the South Pole, within the Antarctic Circle. It is the equivalent to the Arctic (within the Arctic Circle) in the north.

ARCHAEOLOGIST Someone who studies ancient cultures by digging up and examining their remains.

BERING LAND BRIDGE A stretch of land that joined present-day Alaska and eastern Siberia many thousands of years ago. Later, the sea rose over this land and it became the Bering Strait.

CARIBOU The most northerly member of the deer family, which is native to Arctic regions.

EUROPEAN UNION (EU) A grouping of European countries, formerly the European Community, that was formed to improve trade and economic growth.

GLOBAL WARMING An increase in the world's temperatures, thought to be caused in part by polluting gases in the atmosphere.

HARPOON A long, pointed piece of metal that is attached to a cord and thrown to spear whales or other large sea animals.

HUSKIES A breed of dog, often used in the Arctic to pull sledges.

INTESTINES Part of the digestive system of a person or animal.

INUHUIT The name that the Inuit of northwest Greenland call themselves.

INUKTITUT The language spoken by the Inuit of northeastern Alaska, Canada, and Greenland. The rest of Inuits in Alaska and Siberia speak the Yupik language.

KAYAK A canoe-like boat for one or two people using double-bladed paddles.

MISSIONARY Someone who travels around trying to persuade others to join their faith.

MUSK OXEN Stocky animals with large horns and long, dark fur. They are closely related to sheep but look more like cattle.

NARWHAL A small whale with mottled grey skin. The males have a spiral ivory tooth up to 6.5 feet (2 meters) long, like a unicorn of the sea.

OVERHUNT To dramatically reduce animal numbers as a result of hunting.

PERMAFROST A layer of soil that stays below freezing throughout the year.

SHAMAN A spiritual leader who has contact with the spirit world.

SINEW A tough, stringy fiber that attaches muscles to bones.

SMALLPOX A highly infectious disease that included fever and a blistery rash.

TREE LINE The line in the far north past which trees can no longer grow because the ground is permanently frozen.

TUNDRA A frozen area in the Arctic, where mosses and dwarf plants can be seen in the summer.

TUNIQ A name believed to describe the Dorset culture people, who were pushed out of the Arctic by the ancestors of today's Inuit.

INDEX

Web Sites
Due to the changing nature of Internet links, PowerKids Press has developed an online list of Web sites related to the subject of this book. This site is updated regularly. Please use this link to access this list: www.powerkidslinks.com/flash/inuit